Sound at Sight

Saxophone

Book 2
Grades 5-8

by James Rae

Published by
Trinity College London Press Ltd
trinitycollege.com

Registered in England
Company no. 09726123

Copyright © 2007 Trinity College London
Seventh impression, January 2021

Unauthorised photocopying is illegal
No part of this publication may be copied or reproduced in any form or by any means without the prior permission of the publisher.

Printed in England by Caligraving Ltd

Sound at Sight

Sight reading requires you to be able to read and understand music notation, then convert sight into sound and perform a piece. This involves imagining the sound of the music before playing it, which in turn requires familiarity with intervals, chord shapes, rhythmic patterns and textures. The material in this series offers a wide range of examples designed to help players develop their skills and build confidence.

Exam sight reading

In an exam, you have half a minute to prepare your performance. Use this time wisely:

- Check the key and time signatures. You might want to remind yourself of the scale and arpeggio, checking for signs of major or minor first.

- Look for any accidentals, particularly when they apply to more than one note in the bar.

- Set the pace in your head and read through the piece, imagining the sound. It might help to sing part of the music or to clap or tap the rhythm. You can also try out any part of the test if you want to.

- Have you imagined the effect of the dynamics?

When the examiner asks you to play the piece, do not forget the pace you have set. Fluency is more important than anything else: make sure that you keep going whatever happens. If you make a little slip, do not go back and change it. Give a performance of the piece: if you can play the pieces in this book you will be well-prepared, so enjoy the opportunity to play another piece that you didn't know beforehand.

Candidates should always refer to the requirements listed in the most recent syllabus when preparing for an exam.

Grade 5

Semiquavers and the $\frac{6}{8}$ time signature are introduced at Grade 5.

Sound at Sight Saxophone Grade 5

Sound at Sight Saxophone Grade 5

The following examples are also suitable for candidates following the jazz syllabus.

Sound at Sight Saxophone Grade 5

Grade 6

$\frac{3}{8}$ and dotted notes are featured at Grade 6.

1

2

3

Sound at Sight Saxophone Grade 6

Sound at Sight Saxophone Grade 6

The following examples are also suitable for candidates following the jazz syllabus.

7 Slow rock

8 Jazz waltz

9 Slow swing

Sound at Sight Saxophone Grade 6

10

11

12

Sound at Sight Saxophone Grade 7

• Grade 7

Triplets are introduced at this grade.

Sound at Sight Saxophone Grade 7

Sound at Sight Saxophone Grade 7

The following examples are also suitable for candidates following the jazz syllabus.

Sound at Sight Saxophone Grade 8

Grade 8

Changing time signatures and duplets may be included at Grade 8.

Sound at Sight Saxophone Grade 8

The following examples are also suitable for candidates following the jazz syllabus.

Sound at Sight Saxophone Grade 8